THE PURPLE PARACHUTE

Retirement Income to Age One Hundred and Beyond

ANITA FLEGG

THE PURPLE PARACHUTE

RETIREMENT INCOME TO AGE ONE HUNDRED AND BEYOND

Sharp Quill Press
Ottawa, Ontario
Canada

Cover by Donald Lanouette

Library and Archives Canada Cataloguing in Publication

Flegg, Anita, 1960-, author

The Purple Parachute, Retirement Income to Age
One Hundred and Beyond

ISBN 978-0-9812679-2-0 (pbk.)

1. Investing. 2. Investing in real estate. I. Flegg, Anita

Title: The Purple Parachute, Retirement income to age one hundred and beyond

DEDICATION

To my children, Erin and Elizabeth, who, whether I always showed it properly or not, are the most important people in my life.

ACKNOWLEDGEMENTS

Thank you to all of my mentors, teachers, fellow real estate investors, and partners. You have taught me so much. Special thanks to Darren Weeks, Bob Molle, and Matt Donnelly for your advice and suggestions, and especially for pushing me to take on challenges I might not have considered, and then supporting me through them, including writing this book.

Last, but definitely not least, I am so grateful to the members of the Boomer Women Invest Meetup group in Ottawa. Thank you all for allowing me to work on this material with you. Your openness in sharing and questioning is what makes the group work so well.

TABLE OF CONTENTS

FOREWORD

Most of us spend our lives working for our income. But at some point, whether at 21, 43, or 65, most of us want to stop working for money. And whether we retire at 21 or 65, our income probably has to last a long time after that.

> *"The average Canadian retires at age 62 according to Statistics Canada and a 62-year old's life expectancy is age 84. This suggests an average of 22 years of retirement to fund. But not every Canadian is an average Canadian. Some will have much shorter or longer retirements."* Financial Post online (April 2014)

There are four major sources of the income we need to stop working: savings, investments, earnings from a business we own, or inheritance.

In most cases, you need to know something about investing, both to grow your assets, and to turn them into income generators. Common income-generating investments are dividend bearing stocks, rental properties, royalties and businesses.

The purpose of reading books like this is, ultimately, to improve your financial position, and increase the possibility that you will be able to retire someday.

But first you have to realize that it's possible for you. That you are capable of improving your financial situation. That's what context is all about—having the belief that a different situation or outcome is possible. Without that belief, nothing you read, or hear, or learn will make any difference. That's why content—like this book—won't help you unless you have a context large enough to contain the new information.

I met Anita when she joined the Fast Track Mastermind program. As a serious investor, she is always learning, and she has had different coaches and mentors for every stage in her development. She joined our Fast Track program to learn to raise capital successfully—that was the skill she felt she needed next. For Anita, her idea of herself and what was possible needed to grow before she could be successful in raising capital for her projects.

Eighteen months ago when Anita started working with me and the Fast Track team, she discovered that her context needed to be larger to take advantage of all the Fast Track program has to offer, and meet her next group of goals.

I have been impressed with how Anita has embraced the changes and challenges we asked her to take on, and she has been fearless in trying new things, including doing a lot more presentations and public speaking, and pushing herself to open up her context to make her next successes possible.

Do you believe you can make changes that will improve your financial situation? Do you believe you can retire when you want to?

If you answered No, then there is no reason for you to read this book. But if you believe that it is possible to control your own financial fate, then you will find this book informative and interesting.

Anita and I believe that anyone can do it if they believe in themselves, and if they make a point of spending their time with like-minded and positive people.

In this book, Anita concentrates on financial security and investing, especially in rental real estate. Rental real estate is one of the best ways to create additional income, for your current lifestyle or for your retirement.

As my mentor and friend, Robert Kiyosaki, says:

> "Real estate investing, even on a very small scale, remains a tried and true means of building an individual's cash flow and wealth."

What are you waiting for?

— Darren Weeks, Rich Dad Advisor at Robert Kiyosaki, Founder at Fast Track Group, Author of The Art of Raising Capital

Do you need to invest?

Our parents assumed they would retire when they were 65, and they assumed that the government would take care of them for the rest of their lives. Or, if they didn't plan to retire at 65, they were still sure that the government checks would start right on time, on their 65th birthday.

That idea doesn't appeal to me, for several reasons. First, I don't want to wait until I am 65 to stop going to a job every day. Second, I am planning a very busy "second half," and I won't get very far on a government pension. Third, I'm not sure the under-funded government pensions (Canada Pension Plan and Old Age Security) will still be available to me by the time I turn 65.

The bottom line for me is that this plan simply won't do.

My scenario doesn't apply to everyone, and it may not apply to you. You may be working for an employer that provides a pension. You may also be able to retire in your 50s, after 30 or 35 years of teaching or working in the military.

Either way, it's important to ask yourself: "Will I have the income in retirement to live the way I want to live?"

RETIREMENT FUND VS. RETIREMENT INCOME

When I was in my 20s and 30s, I believed in the conventional wisdom: If I amassed a retirement fund of one million dollars, it would generate enough income to support me indefinitely. Watching prices rise and interest rates fall made me wonder about this, and as I entered my 40s, this no longer seemed likely.

One of the first things—and I think one of the most important things—I learned when I started studying money and investing, is that is more useful and more important to plan for income than for a nest egg. The one million dollar fund I was planning in my 30s might generate plenty of income some years, but depending on how it was invested, it could leave me short in other years.

Now I plan for income, so I choose investments that generate the kind of income I need for the retirement lifestyle I am planning.

There are many kinds of investments you could make, and the distinction between income-generating investments and non-income-generating investments may not be obvious, so consider the following investments you might own, or you might be considering.

- Your home – No income
- Your home with a basement suite – Income
- Cottage/summer home – No income
- Summer home/Cottage (rented out) - Income
- Stocks – No income

- Stocks (with dividend) – Income
- Mutual funds – No income
- Real estate (rental) – Income (when purchased correctly)
- Real estate (development land) – No income
- Real estate (farm land) – Income (when rented to a farmer)

Keep in mind that while you are working, you may not need the income, so you may choose to reinvest all of the growth. This means that your investment fund grows more quickly.

HOW MUCH MONEY DO YOU NEED TO RETIRE?

An easy way to figure out how much income you will need to retire is to look at your current lifestyle and compare it to the lifestyle you have planned for your retirement.

To do this, you need to know how you want to retire.

If you are planning to retire to the same lifestyle you have now; for instance, living in the same house, driving the same car, doing the same activities, and sticking to one or two vacation trips each year, your cost of living after retirement may be similar to your current cost of living. If this is the case, you can easily conclude that your retirement income will need to be very similar to your current income. You may spend less on work-type clothing and vehicle expenses, but you may spend more on leisure activities and travel.

On the other hand, if you plan to spend the first decade of your retirement travelling the world in five-star style, your retirement income may have to be higher than your current income.

You might decide to sell your home and retire to Nicaragua (for example), in which case you are likely to be able to cut your income requirements to half of what it currently costs you to live in Canada.

Or you may be planning never to fully retire. If you love your work, and you don't plan to ever fully stop, then you may continue to have some work income until you are 85 or 90.

There is no right or wrong way to retire or not retire; the point is that you need to make a plan. You won't know how much income you will need until you know how you will be spending your time. And you won't be able to choose the proper investments until you know what income you will need.

DO YOU NEED TO CHANGE HOW YOU ARE INVESTING?

If you already know how you want to spend your retirement, and you already know you will have the income to retire to the lifestyle you want, then you may want to put down this book, and spend your day doing something else.

Before you go, though; one more question: Is your money working hard for you? Is it growing as it should be?

If your investments are bringing in less than two or three

percent per year, then you should definitely consider re-investing your money to get your returns above the inflation rate. If your returns are lower than the inflation rate, then you are effectively losing money every year, and that's not good for your retirement income.

At the very least, it will be worth your time to examine your current investments, and perform the income/no-income test on each one. If you have a company or government-sponsored pension, you may not currently have any control over how the fund is invested, but look at it anyway, and ask questions until you understand how it is invested, and how it will be paid out. It may be perfect, or it may not allow for any control at all, but either way, you may be able to improve your outcomes using one or more of the strategies in this book.

For non-pension investments, make sure they are actually making money. Consider those mutual funds your financial advisor sold you. I have had people tell me that they are making an 8% return (or even more) in their mutual funds. When I have asked more questions, though, I learned that they made 8% in the past year, but over the life of the investment, they have broken even, or even lost money. Often, this 8% is also calculated before the management funds are paid, and in Canada, these fees can cost up to 2%, reducing your return to 6%.

More about mutual funds, and why they are often a poor investment, as we continue.

MAKING A PLAN

The first thing to do when making your retirement plan is to look at where you are now. Open a spreadsheet program or get a clean sheet of lined paper, and write the following column titles along the top.

- Investment
- Investment type (rental real estate, mutual fund, gold/silver)
- Financial institution (Scotia Bank, for example, but it may not apply)
- Investment value
- Monthly income
- Availability date (for LIRA and pensions)

Fill in the table with all the investments you currently have. Based on the income you previously determined you will need for your planned retirement lifestyle, will you have enough monthly income?

If nothing changes, will this income be sufficient at your retirement date?

What return do you need on your current holdings to get there by 60? By 65? By 55?

IF YOU DON'T HAVE WHAT YOU NEED...

Don't despair if your spreadsheet shows a picture that is less rosy than you had hoped. By creating this simple status sheet, you are already miles ahead of most people, who typically ignore the whole question and hope for the best.

First, consider the amount you are putting aside each paycheck to add to your assets. Are you adding enough each year to get you to where you need to be before retiring?

If you are not adding any money to your investments on a monthly basis, how much money do you need to be investing each month?

IF YOU INVEST, WHAT HAVE YOU TRIED SO FAR?

When I ask people what they invest in, many people say they invest in their RRSP.

RRSP stands for Registered Retirement Savings Plan, and it is defined as, "a savings plan for individuals which allows them to defer tax on money to be used for retirement".

It's a savings plan, not an investment, so the next question is, what investments are you holding in your RRSP?

The Canada Revenue Agency allows you to hold the following investments in your RRSP:

- Stocks and mutual funds
- Bonds and debentures
- Term deposits and Guaranteed Investment Certificates
- Gold and silver certificates
- Mortgages secured by Real property (Canadian property only)

If you haven't made a decision about what to invest in, then your RRSP may be sitting in your account as cash, and earning nothing. This is no better than putting your savings under your mattress. (Actually it's worse — your mattress doesn't charge fees!). Don't let fear paralyze you; study and ask successful people what they do.

A WORD ABOUT TAKING INVESTMENT ADVICE

Most people don't know what to invest in, so they allow the bank or financial institution sales person to talk them into their "default" investments, usually mutual funds.

Before allowing anyone to talk you into any investment, whether mutual fund or something else, ask them these questions:

> *"Is this what you are personally invested in? And if so, will this investment produce enough for you to retire on schedule?"*

> *"If not, what do you invest in?"*

I think it's pretty obvious what the right and wrong answers are. You may find that the sales representative is reluctant to answer, and that tells you something useful, too. Actually, these are good questions to ask anyone who is trying to talk you into investing in anything at all.

Most people also talk to family and friends for investing advice. This is great if you know someone who is a professional investor, but in most cases, your family and friends will be repeating what their investment advisor told them—they may not even understand it themselves.

Instead, talk to a professional investor, or better yet, two or three professional investors. Ask them what they invest in, and why, and ask them how to choose a good investment, when investing in their specialty.

I know this is more work than you normally do when choosing investments for your RRSP, so ask yourself these questions:

"How important is it to have my RRSP grow?"

"How important is it not to lose money?"

Remember, it's better to leave your money in cash than to buy a losing investment. Take the time to do your research—starting with this book—before buying any investment.

WHAT HAS WORKED TO INCREASE YOUR RESOURCES AND WHAT HASN'T WORKED?

Make a list of the investments you have purchased over the years. Beside each one, mark whether it grew or lost money. Every investment brochure will remind you that past performance is not necessarily a good predictor of future performance, but they will all tout their history of good returns, anyway.

If you don't know how well each investment performed or is performing, dig up your statements, and compare your initial investment(s) with the current value of the investment.

If you have made money, great! Is this investment likely to continue to grow? Is this something you can realistically evaluate on your own?

If not, then ask someone who will be able to help you figure it out. Just don't ask the person who sold the investment to you. This question puts them in a conflict of interest position. They know you will move your money if the answer is No. Even if the investment has lost money, your bank sales person is sure to tell you that the investment is most certainly on the upswing.

If your investment is losing money, then you need to decide whether it is time to sell the investment and find a new place to put your money.

Very simple, but you'd be surprised to learn how many people sit on losing investments, hoping they will recover, usually because they have no idea what to do instead.

INVESTING MYTHS

As with many areas of knowledge, investing "knowledge" is full of myth:

Risk must go up with return: The riskiest investments are those you don't understand. If you don't understand what you are investing in, ask. The better you understand the investment, how it works, how the profits are created, and what the potential problems are, the less risky the investment will be for you.

Mutual funds are safe: Mutual funds are the default investment because that's what the bank has to offer, and it is another way for them to make money. This doesn't mean that the particular fund they are recommending is making money, or breaking even.

Remember, it is usually the investor who is risky. Or put another way, it is the investor's lack of knowledge that makes an investment risky.

A LAST WORD ABOUT MUTUAL FUNDS

As you will already have noticed, I am not a fan of mutual funds. Here are the main reasons:

1. Mutual funds are sold by sales people, not financial experts. The mutual funds are often recommended for you based on what the bank wants to sell, not what's best for you.

2. Most people are afraid to buy stocks because they don't know how to evaluate the various companies. The mutual fund is just a bundle of stocks that someone has chosen. Investing in a mutual fund means you are investing in a whole basket of stocks you don't understand, rather than just one.

3. Canada has the highest mutual fund management fees in the world, and they can add 2% or more. Even if your mutual fund produces a decent return over a period of time, remember to subtract at least 2% before you get too excited about all the money you are making.

The financial institution and your sales person make money on your mutual fund, even when it is dropping in value. This is why they will try to talk you out of moving your money, even when it is dropping in value.

Don't get me wrong. Your mutual fund salesperson is probably a very nice person who thinks they are giving you good advice—I know mine were. They are simply not very knowledgeable about investing in general, and they are doing their work to make money, as we all are. They are also bound, by regulation, to advice generated by your answers to a questionnaire about risk and goals. They are not actually allowed to recommend an investment other than the one their software spits out.

Security First

Saving and investing are very important, and for many of us, it's the only way we will ever be able to retire, but the best laid plans are sometimes derailed by illness, disability or premature job loss.

WHAT IF YOU BECOME ILL OR LOSE YOUR JOB BEFORE YOU ARE READY?

Most of us have very little cushion, and most of us would have trouble managing for even a month or two without our salary.

While putting aside money for investing, you should also be putting aside savings that you keep in cash, ready for emergencies. Keep an emergency fund that makes you comfortable, but the minimum should be three or four month's salary, at a minimum.

If you've read Rich Dad Poor Dad, you will know that Robert Kiyosaki recommends contributing to three piggy banks before you spend your take-home pay on anything else. The three "piggy banks" are labelled:

Savings: This is the savings account that will save you in the case of job loss or illness that prevents you from working. This should be at least three or four month's salary.

Investing: This money will be used to buy your first investment or more investments.

Giving: This is for charitable giving. Helping others should always be high on our list of priorities, and automating charitable giving just makes sense. This can be done through a monthly debit that you have authorized your favourite charity to take, or by saving until a certain amount is reached, prompting you to write a check to your charity, or both.

Rather than using physical piggy banks, I use online savings accounts, and I have set up automatic transfers to these accounts each pay period.

Having this automated saving, investing and giving system set up will give you peace of mind, and a feeling of control over your financial life.

CRITICAL ILLNESS AND DISABILITY INSURANCE

While your savings account will keep you going for three or four months, what if you develop a long-term illness or disability that keeps you from returning to work?

This is where the right insurance can take care of you until your retirement plan kicks in.

Start by finding an independent insurance broker, and ask about the various types of income replacement insurance policies. Your broker can help you find the right policies and coverage values, based on your budget and the particular risks you are most worried about.

I strongly recommend that you find an independent broker.

Many brokers work for a specific company, so they can only sell you insurance policies offered by that company. An independent broker can search the universe of policies to find the products that will meet your needs.

DO YOU HAVE A WILL?

Having a will has nothing to do with investing, but it makes things much easier at your death. It also ensures that your assets are distributed as YOU want them distributed, rather than relying on the defaults built into Canadian and provincial law.

This is even more important if you have businesses and/or real estate, or if you have no husband or wife to whom your estate will automatically go.

I have a will and an estate plan because I want to be sure that my real estate portfolio will go to my daughters in a way that works best for them. Because they are young—in their 20s— I also want to make sure that dealing with my estate is as easy as I can make it. This planning includes buying life insurance to cover various costs they will run into.

LIFE INSURANCE

Life insurance is not mandatory, unless you have someone who depends on you for support. But even if you have no dependants, it may be helpful to have enough insurance to cover funeralexpenses, especially when you consider that most of your assets will be locked up for some time after your death.

Another reason to have life insurance is to make transition of your business easier. Upon your death, there will be taxes to pay, and legal fees to cover. If you have investment real estate, for example, capital gains tax will kick in immediately, so you may want to have insurance that will cover the capital gains tax so that your executor doesn't have to put property up for sale right away.

Another reason to have life insurance is for properties and corporations that you own with partners. If a partner dies, their share may be willed to their beneficiaries. If you don't want to worry about suddenly having an inexperienced partner, then it may be wise to have life insurance on all of the partners to pay out to the business or partnership so that you can buy out their beneficiaries in the event of their death.

For me, life insurance is mostly about making life as easy as possible for my executors and partners.

Why Real Estate

In keeping with the "understand what you invest in" admonition, I don't invest in stocks and bonds. This is entirely because I have not yet put in the time to invest well. I owned stocks in the past, but I lost most of my money because I didn't know what I was doing, and I invested emotionally. If you want to invest in stocks and bonds, please get some training, help and advice (from experts who are NOT trying to sell you on anything).

What primarily attracts me to real estate is that it is a physical investment that I can see, touch, and smell. It's concrete, and has real practical value that is easy to understand.

Investing in gold and silver is attractive to me for the same reasons, and I do hold some, but real estate is particularly attractive because real estate also generates income that I can live on.

Investing in gold and silver requires special knowledge, too, so you should study it before jumping in. I recommend starting with Michael Moloney's Guide to Investing in Gold and Silver.

The point here is not to tell you what to invest in. The point is that the greatest risk comes from investing in assets you don't understand well. The most profit, and the least risk, comes when you study, and really learn, the asset class you are investing in.

I have been studying and investing in real estate, specifically, rental properties, so that's what the bulk of this book is about.

ADVANTAGES OF REAL ESTATE AS AN INVESTMENT

There are many advantages to real estate as an investment. As I list them, ask yourself whether buying stocks, (or mutual funds), offers the same advantages.

Leverage: Just as when you bought your home with a five or ten percent down payment, you can buy rental real estate with only a fraction of the purchase price as down payment. The really attractive part is that you gain from 100% of the property, and you get to keep 100% of the profits, even though you may have spent only 20% or less to buy the property.

Control of Value: You have no control over the value of your stocks, but you can control the value of your real estate properties. You can increase the value by improving the building or the grounds, or by adding to the structure—adding a garage, for example. Even something as simple and inexpensive as new paint often increases the value of a property. Note that neglecting the property has an effect on the value, too, and your property can lose a lot of its value if you allow it to become run-down.

Another way to increase the value of your property may be by tearing it down and building something better, by changing the use of the land or the buildings on it, or even by just rezoning it.

Value will never go to zero: A property's value (almost) never goes to zero. I suppose there are circumstances in which a property can lose all its value (becoming a giant sink hole or ending up under water permanently, or becoming extremely contaminated), but it's not a common event, and it's rarely permanent.

Banks will lend on it: Lenders love to lend on real estate for the same reasons I like it—it's a concrete asset that has an intrinsic value. They can also repossess the property if the borrower stops paying on the loan (mortgage), and sell it to recover their money.

The value changes slowly: Unlike stocks, which fluctuate daily or even hourly, and which require constant attention, property values change slowly, and in a predictable cyclical fashion. This allows the investor time to plan and reflect on possible improvements or whether it is time to sell.

Many ways to profit from owning real estate: There are seven profit centres in each piece of real estate you own, and this is another huge reason that real estate is such an attractive investment type. The profit centres are discussed in detail in the next section.

There are also a couple of disadvantages in owning real estate, and we must mention them as well. Education, preparation, and good management are the best ways to counteract these disadvantages.

Not liquid: When you are invested in real estate (or mortgages) your funds are not liquid. It can take quite a bit of time to get your money back out of the property, depending on the resale market at the time.

Requires a high level of knowledge: To be successful in real estate investing, you need to have done your homework. Just some of the things you need to study include your particular market, the real estate cycle, how to attract and retain good tenants, tenant laws in the province, mortgages and insurance, and probably construction and maintenance. According to some business sources, real estate requires the highest level of knowledge of all the investment types, with the sole exception of starting and running a business.

Changes are slow: This is a plus and a minus. The value of real estate properties changes slowly, and it takes time to buy and sell it. This allows lots of time for course correction.

REAL ESTATE PROFIT CENTRES

One of the most attractive features of real estate investing is that there are so many ways to profit from it when it is well-managed. Here are the seven profit centers available to you with real estate:

Equity: As with most aspects of real estate, this may take some work and some specialized market knowledge, but you can often purchase real estate with additional equity built in. As an example, you might find a property worth $650,000, and you are able to negotiate a purchase price of $600,000. This gives you starting equity of $50,000. This happens more often than you might imagine, especially for investors who have taken the time to learn their market, and who are always looking at and for properties.

Principle pay down: Just as with your home mortgage, the mortgage payment includes an interest portion and a principal portion. As you pay principal, your mortgage owing is reduced. The bonus with rental properties is that the tenants, by paying rent, pay the mortgage and all the expenses.

This is not guaranteed, of course; if you pay too much for the property, then the rents may not be enough to cover all the expenses, and you may have to put in money for operating expenses every year.

Cash flow: When you buy rental real estate well, there will be money left over after paying all the expenses, (mortgage, taxes, insurance, and maintenance). The left-over money is the cash flow, which is sometimes called the profit.

Earned appreciation: Earned appreciation is the increase in property value that you create by improving the property. This is sometimes called Forced appreciation. You can increase the value of the property in many ways, from paint and landscaping, all the way to major renovations or additions.

Another way to improve the property is to change its use. An example of this is getting the property rezoned and replacing a single family home with a multi-unit building. Some real estate investors specialize in converting apartment buildings into condominiums, which is another way to increase the value, often by several times.

Market appreciation: Over time, many real estate properties rise in value, year over year, in many areas in Canada, especially in areas where the job market is hot. A current example is Alberta, and particularly Calgary, where prices have risen significantly as people move in for the jobs. This is market appreciation.

You should not assume that there will be market appreciation. Some markets will drop, and your best chance of benefiting from market appreciation is to do your homework, and study your market before buying.

Tax deductions: When you own rental real estate for the purpose of making a profit, the Canada Revenue Agency (CRA) allows you to deduct all of the expenses you incur in operating the property. Hire a good book-keeper and accountant to make sure that you are taking all of the deductions that are allowed, and none that aren't allowed.

Depreciation: Depreciation is a Canada Revenue Agency creation that allows an additional tax deduction for rental properties. When you sell the property, all of this depreciation must be repaid to the tax department. Whether or not to claim this deduction is something you need to discuss with your accountant.

As you can see, there are many ways a savvy real estate investor can make money in rental real estate. I hope it is also clear to you that you need a lot of education and a good team of professionals to do well in active real estate investing.

In the next chapter, we will discuss some ways to invest in real estate more passively. Investing passively means spending less time learning the detailed ins and outs of real estate investing and management, while still benefiting from the real estate profit centres.

Ways to invest in Real Estate

T here are many ways to invest in real estate. At the active end of the spectrum, investing in real estate requires a lot of time and a lot of real estate knowledge, while at the other end of the spectrum, you just need to know how to find and evaluate trustworthy real estate investors and investments.

This chapter describes the various ways to take advantage of the great returns possible with investment properties.

All real estate investments are also somewhere between completely passive and busily active.

ACTIVE INVESTING

Active investing requires the most knowledge and the highest level of work. When you invest actively, you are doing the research, finding the property, getting the financing, completing the purchase, and then managing the property.

Active investing may also include finding investors who will participate by providing the down payment or by lending the mortgage.

Only a small percentage of investors have the time or inclination to be active investors. The greatest proportion of real estate investors, by far, do not want to be active investors, so they lend their money to, or partner with, active investors.

PASSIVE INVESTING

There are many ways to invest passively in real estate; here are the broad categories.

REAL ESTATE INVESTMENT TRUST (REIT)

A REIT is the closest you can get to a stock, while still investing in real estate properties. There are many REITs in Canada, both public and private.

In general, each REIT specializes in one type of property. The general categories are:

- Residential, usually apartment buildings
- Malls, Retail and Strip Malls
  Office buildings
- Healthcare, which includes properties like long term care homes
- Industrial
- Hotels
- Farmland
- Timberland

Some REITs invest in combinations of these general types. REITs purchase properties they believe will provide cash flow, and appreciate in value over time.

Sometimes you will be offered investment opportunities, both inside and outside REITs, that are speculative. What I mean is that you will be asked to put your money into something that does not yet exist. When investing in land and projects under development, your investment is not generating any income, so if something goes wrong, there will be no way to pay you returns, and you may also be at risk of losing your investment. This is an advanced investment type that is recommended only for very experienced real estate investors. If you are a beginner, I recommend that you invest elsewhere for now.

One of the strengths of REITs is that the profits come from the combination of the all of the properties being held. In a REIT that is performing well, the profitable properties outnumber the properties that are not profitable.

Another strength is that you can invest with a relatively small amount of money, generally much less than you would need to buy a rental property yourself. You are pooling your investment money with that of many other investors, and you are all buying properties together.

When you buy shares in a REIT, you are buying into a group of properties. You won't know which specific buildings your money is going into. Later in this book, we will talk about what makes a good property purchase, but this kind of analysis doesn't apply when you purchase shares in a REIT.

There are public and private REITs. Both public and private REITs have a board of directors and a management team. Private REITs can be purchased directly from the REIT sales team, and possibly some brokers who work with the REIT.

Publically traded REITs are the same, except you can buy and sell them on the Toronto Stock Exchange (TSX) or the New York Stock Exchange (NYSE), for example.

As with every investment vehicle, REITs have advantages and disadvantages.

Advantages:

REITs are completely hands-off investments, so while you are investing in rental real estate, with all of the advantages real estate provides, you don't have to deal with tenants or property problems.

REITs, especially publically-traded REITs, are liquid investments. You can sell them at any time while the markets are open. You can also buy with relatively low amounts of money.

Investing in REITs does not require that you understand the details of real estate investing. After confirming the experience and integrity of the REIT management, you don't need to know much more to invest. In fact, you won't have the opportunity to analyze individual properties—the information will not usually be available to you, except in aggregate or possibly, in examples.

Disadvantages:

REITs are highly regulated, and with private REITs, there are restrictions on who can invest, and how much they can invest. Many investments are available only to accredited investors, which means that, depending on your income and net worth, there may be a minimum investment amount.

Many REITs look very official, and everyone you talk to will be wearing a suit, but before investing in one, do your research and talk to a lot of people to make sure the REIT is well-managed and has a profitable business model.

No matter who you invest with, the most important attributes to look for are experience and integrity; make sure the people running the REIT know what they are doing, and that they are trustworthy.

LENDING MONEY TO ACTIVE INVESTORS

Active real estate investors are always looking for money for their projects, and they are often willing to pay very good interest rates on the money. Sometimes they need the money for a few years, while sometimes, they need the money only for a few months. Lending your money, both long term and short term, can be very lucrative.

When you lend money to a real estate investor, you do not share in the profits of the property. You make money by charging interest on the sum you lend.

There are two ways to lend your money to active investors — through mortgages or promissory notes.

Mortgages: Lending as a mortgage is the safest way to lend money because a mortgage is a legal agreement that must be registered by a lawyer. A mortgage is a legal way of ensuring that your loan is secured by collateral—the property itself. When a mortgage is registered on the property, you have the right to take the property (foreclose) if you aren't getting your payments, or the full sum is not returned to you on time. This is advantageous to you as a lender, as it gives you added security. Another nice thing about lending mortgage funds is that you can require the borrower to pay all of your legal fees.

On the other side of the equation, borrowers/real estate investors are willing to do all this work and pay all these fees only if the loan amount and the deal returns are large enough to support the additional costs. Or if they are desperate. I'm sure I don't need to tell you to stay away from desperate borrowers.

Promissory note: A promissory note is simply a promise to pay. In its simplest form, a promissory note is an IOU. I don't recommend lending your money on an IOU, but your lawyer will be able to provide a promissory note contract for you to use, if you choose to make this type of loan. Just as the IOU your brother-in-law gave you is not worth the paper it's printed on, the same risk is a factor with promissory note. You can protect yourself by checking the credentials and references of the borrower, and by making sure the property you are lending on actually exists. You may also pay your lawyer to register the promissory note on the property's title. This will not give you foreclosure rights if the borrower stops paying, but it does ensure that you are notified if the borrower tries to sell the property so that you can stop the sale, or make sure that you are paid out of the sale proceeds. You would also have the option of suing.

Promissory notes are good for short term loans, especially in small amounts, when you are very comfortable with the integrity of the borrower.

Active investors may be individuals or institutions. There are the local individual real estate investors you meet at your real estate club, and there are also firms like Fortress Real Capital (this is not an endorsement, only an example), who raise money for large building projects, and pool the money of many investors to create a large second mortgage (syndicated mortgage).

Research, research, and research some more before committing your investment funds to anyone, no matter how official and professional they look.

JOINT VENTURES

You can invest in joint ventures, also with active real estate investors. A joint venture, also called a JV, can be a passive investment or an active one, depending on how you and your co-venturer(s) set it up.

Rather than just being paid interest, as with lending down

payment or mortgage funds, in most joint ventures, you will share in the profits. Keep in mind that you will also share in the losses.

A joint venture is an agreement with one or more other investors. In the real estate world, there is generally a primary active real estate investor—the person who finds the property and pulls together the deal—and one or more money partners.

Just as the mortgage has a mortgage agreement, and a promissory note has its agreement, joint ventures are enforced using joint venture agreements.

There are as many joint venture options as there are people investing. Any combination of contributions—money, mortgage and management work—are OK, as long as all of the partners agree.

The joint venture agreement should contain the answers to the all of the Who-does-what and What-if questions that could come up.

There is a lot more detail about what should be in a joint venture agreement in the Joint Venture chapter later in the book; for now just note that joint ventures are one of the many ways you can invest in real estate.

JOINT VENTURES – INVESTING MONEY ONLY

At the passive end of joint venture possibilities, you will provide the down payment or a portion of it, and you may also be asked to provide extra cash for renovations or for use as a contingency fund.

The money will be your only contribution. You may or may not be asked for your opinion on the big decisions, depending on what's written in your joint venture agreement.

The JV agreement will also define how much and how often you will be paid, and in what proportion, and how the profits are shared when the property is sold.

JOINT VENTURES – INVESTING TIME AND MONEY

At the other end of the JV continuum, you could be the person finding and purchasing the property, or you could be in charge of managing the property.

There are dozens of options, and as long as all of the responsibilities are covered, each co-venturer can be as involved or as uninvolved as they like. Profit-sharing usually reflects the perceived value of each co-venturer's contribution.

DUE DILIGENCE

No matter what the investment, you must do all the checking yourself. Many investment advisors and investment sales people don't expect you to ask all of the questions you should ask, and they know you would rather trust them than do the work yourself. I understand—it's not the fun part—but this is the minimum checking you should do. And as you get the answers, trust your common sense. If the answers and explanations sound fishy, they probably are.

The two most important questions, in all cases:

1. Does the organization or investor have experience in the investment category? Have they been successful?
2. Is the organization or investor trustworthy? Ask for references, or if that isn't possible, search the internet for reviews, good and bad.

Next, examine the investment itself.

1. Do the numbers make sense? Do the promised returns make sense? Do they look probable?
2. What are the risks? What is the worst case scenario? If the worst happens, can you live with the consequences? (No matter how good the investment seems, never invest money you can't afford to lose.)

BE CAREFUL WHOSE ADVICE YOU LISTEN TO.

Everyone has an opinion, but most people aren't experienced or educated investors. When people around you give you advice, ask yourself these questions:

1. Does he/she have knowledge in this area? Has he/she made investments like this?
2. Has he/she had a bad experience that might taint all opportunities he/she sees?

3. What does he/she have to gain or lose if you invest, or don't invest?

Examples:

Your investment advisor says it's a bad idea: Your investment advisor may or may not be experienced in the investment you are looking at, but he/she has a vested interest—your investment advisor doesn't want to lose your business, and his or her income.

Your Mom/Dad/Sister/Brother/Aunt/Uncle says it's a bad idea: Your family wants to protect you, especially from things they may be afraid of themselves. Most people tend to be uneasy about things they are unfamiliar with. And when people are nervous or uncertain, they almost always say No.

The bottom line is that you should be respectful of the opinions of others, but also look at them critically. Try to understand why they might feel the way they do, and then decide for yourself whether their opinion should be relevant for your decision.

Joint Ventures

The joint venture agreement should contain the answers to the all of the Who-does-what and What-if questions. Keep in mind that the following is not an exhaustive list—any current or potential set of conditions relevant to your group of investors or the property or properties you are investing in should be covered explicitly in the JV agreement.

- Who will supply the down payment? Who will supply the contingency and the renovation money (if applicable)?

- Who will qualify for the mortgage?

- Who will manage the property renovations?

- Who will be on the management team? Who will manage the property (tenants, repairs, maintenance, snow and grass, etc.)?

- How often is money paid out to the co-venturers, and in what proportions? How much money must stay in the account to cover emergencies?

- When will the property be sold? What are the conditions for selling the property, and who decides?

- When the property is sold, how are the proceeds divided between/among the co-venturers?

- When money has to be spent, which partners have authority to spend it?

- When is approval by the whole group required for decisions—monetary and other? Is there any money limit or jurisdictional limit on the decision-making power of the management team?

- What happens if there is a major problem affecting the property that requires an infusion of cash? Who must supply the money?

- What happens if a partner wants to leave the joint venture before the property is sold? (Most real estate joint venture agreements assume that the joint venture agreement terminates at the sale of the asset, but other options are possible, as long as all the co-venturers agree.)

- What happens if there is a cash call, and a partner refuses to pay his or her share? (A cash call is the situation in which additional money is required to keep the venture going, and cash is required from one or more of the co-venturers.)

- What happens if a partner dies? Does the share of the asset get purchased by one or more of the co-venturers? Does the share of the asset go to the beneficiaries?

As you can see, there are many possibilities to cover, even in the simplest arrangement with the most congenial of co-venturers.

Choosing and running your Real Estate investment

I f you are investing on your own, or you are the lead person on a joint venture project, your primary activities will be finding and running the investment property or properties.

In some ways, investing in real estate seems easy, especially for those of us who have purchased our own homes. Many of us also know people who have rented out their basement or cottage, or own one rental property.

Almost invariably, people who have rented their basement or who own one other house have jumped into being a landlord without any study or research, and their property may or not make any money. Often, tenants are referred to them or, if they advertise, they accept the first tenant that seems to have a job.

In other words, for many people, real estate is a sideline or hobby, and is not run as a business. Without a plan, this can go badly, and we all know people who tried it, and now "hate real estate".

Although owning real estate as a sideline can work reasonably well if you own one or two properties, and you are just looking to sell when you are ready to retire, you are unlikely to be able to scale up to more properties successfully without some education and a business approach to rental real estate.

You might have no interest in scaling up to multiple rental properties, but whether you own one property or you own many and plan to someday own 100 or more, it is important to learn all you can about acquiring and running investment properties.

In this chapter, we will walk through how to approach your purchase, and how to get it running smoothly after you own the property.

WHAT TO LOOK FOR

What makes a good purchase? Ultimately, a good purchase has several important attributes:

It's in a neighbourhood where people want to live: Ideal investment neighbourhoods are safe, and have easy access to places people work and go to school. They have easy access to public transportation.

It's in a neighbourhood that you are comfortable in, and that attracts the kind of tenants you will be happy to work with: You may be able to get a good price on a property in a bad area, but if you are frequently having to find new tenants because the area is dangerous, or you are constantly having to make repairs because of vandalism, then this property may not be a good choice for you.

Every investor is different. Some don't mind doing the extra work entailed in renting to students; some are comfortable with renting to people who are on social assistance; and some investors work only with short-term executive rentals. I recommend starting with properties that are attractive to middle-class families. This is the easiest demographic to work with, and a good way to start developing your property management skills.

There are jobs nearby, so that when your tenant leaves, you will easily find another tenant: Because tenants must have jobs (with the exception of those tenants on social assistance), your property must be accessible to where the jobs are. This is why the best rentals are in urban areas. In the larger urban areas, your tenant may not have to move to find another job. This is the best case, since getting a new tenant is much more expensive than keeping the (cooperative and paying) tenant you have.

There will still be jobs nearby in 5-10 years, or however long you intend to hold the property: This is a good reason to buy in a stable or growing urban area. If the jobs are moving or likely to move out of the area, your tenants will leave, too. Without tenants, your property will be a drain on your finances rather than a source of income.

The property can be purchased for a price that will allow positive cash flow: Unless you want to contribute personally to the property bank account every month, you need to look for a property for which the rents will cover all the costs, plus provide a little extra. This "little extra" will contribute to your income. How to do these calculations is explained later in the book.

You may have heard real estate investors say, rather cryptically, that you make your money "when you buy". What they mean is that they follow the rules explained in this section to ensure that they make money through the life of the investment. They also do their best to buy properties under market value, so that they start out with equity in the property.

The next few sections provide a few more things to know before taking the plunge.

TYPES OF INVESTMENT PROPERTIES

A single family home or duplex is a good way to start your investment portfolio. These are the easiest to buy and manage, and the easiest deals to understand. These are also the easiest to sell, when the time comes. But there are many kinds of rental properties you can invest in.

Residential multiplexes

This class of property ranges from triplexes (three apartments) all the way up to big apartment complexes that contain hundreds of apartments. These are divided into two categories, residential and commercial.

Residential multiplexes contain up to about five apartments. They are financed in the same way as single family homes, in that your good credit is required for the purchase. The purchase process is very similar to the process you use to buy your own home.

Commercial multiplexes contain more than five apartments, and they are financed differently. Financing on commercial multis does not necessarily hinge on your own credit (although you will still likely have to provide personal guarantees), since lenders are much more interested in the income the property will produce. Financing is also different in that lenders usually won't lend 80% of the purchase price (Loan-to-value, or LTV), as they routinely do for small residential properties. Usually the lender will agree to lend between 50-65% of the purchase price, so you will need a much higher down payment.

There are many more requirements for closing the purchase of a large multi. In addition to the building inspection, which you should ALWAYS do for every property you are considering buying, lenders require environmental inspections as well. I won't go into detail here, but there are two things you need to know about environmental studies. First, they can be expensive—although you can negotiate to share the cost with the seller—and second, there are three phases of environmental inspection.

In the Phase I environmental study, you retain an engineering firm to research the history of the property to try to determine whether there is any possibility that the property could be contaminated with oil or other toxic substances. They research the property records and look at historical aerial photographs of the property, if they are available, to determine whether there might ever have been oil tanks on the property. You might discover, for example, that the property was a gas station or a farm operation in a previous life.

If the Phase I report results in any doubt at all, then you commission a Phase II environmental study. In this Phase, core samples are taken from the property, and tested for toxic compounds. If the tests don't reveal any problems, then you are done. If toxic compounds are found in one or more samples, then an environmental cleanup must be performed. This cleanup is referred to as Environmental Phase III.

A few years ago, we purchased a building that had to be taken all the way to Phase III; the parking lot had to be dug up and all the soil replaced. This delayed closing, and when all was said and done, the closing took six months to complete, but I was glad to know the property was now clear of oil, with the reports to prove it.

Not only are you adding the expense of environmental studies, legal expenses are higher when closing a purchase of this type, because the purchase contract is usually more complex. You will also be booking and paying for the building appraisal. You must use an appraiser who is approved by the lender, so if they don't volunteer a list of approved appraisers, ask for it to make sure that you don't end up paying for two appraisals.

There are also lender fees to pay. In the purchase of a house or small multi-plex, the lender may not charge lender fees, and they will probably also pay your mortgage broker. When financing a commercial building of any kind, the lender charges fees, and you also have to pay your mortgage broker directly. This is different than purchasing small residential buildings—for the small buildings, the lender pays the mortgage broker.

Commercial buildings

Commercial properties have commercial tenants rather than residential tenants. In some ways, commercial buildings are easier to manage, since you are bound only by the commercial lease; you don't have to worry about the rules and requirements of the landlord tenant board in your province.

All of the lender rules discussed in the Commercial multis section also apply here. All the expenses, including the increased down payment, the lender fees and the environmental studies must be included in your budget when buying commercial buildings, too.

Legal fees may even be a bit higher, since you should have your lawyer review the tenant leases to make sure that there is nothing in the agreements that will give you grief later. In one building we looked at, a review of the lease (there was only one business tenant) showed that we would not be able to raise the rent for ten years. Since the building currently provided very little cash flow, and expenses always go up, this was a showstopper for us, and we didn't buy the building.

Small businesses

Some attractive small businesses you might be looking at include laundromats, car washes, and self-storage properties. In each of these, you have all of the work and expense of closing a commercial property, as discussed in the previous section, plus you must analyse the business itself to make sure it is viable, or you can make it viable. I strongly recommend using the services of an experienced business accountant in analyzing the business.

Building and environmental inspections will have to be done, and it will also be wise to hire a specialist in the particular business to examine the facility and equipment to make sure you aren't surprised by failing equipment or regulatory requirements after purchasing the building.

There is a great deal more to know about buying a business, and I strongly recommend that you talk to experienced business people and get legal advice before buying any business.

WHAT YOU NEED BEFORE YOU BUY

When considering any new property purchase, you must be prepared with these three main things.

Down payment: In the case of residential properties, you need a minimum of 20% of the purchase price. There are no guarantees, though. I once had a lender suddenly reduce their lending offer to 65% LTV on a single-family home I was buying. With the federal government changing the mortgage rules so frequently, lenders have become quite skittish. In the case of commercial properties, whether large residential or commercial tenants, always have a plan for at least 35% down payment. (Before you put this book down in a panic over finding down payment funds, I describe many options for getting the funds in a later chapter.)

Credit score: In any borrowing situation, prospective lenders will review your credit report. For standard residential purposes, the credit score of the borrower has to be at least 680. This varies a bit from lender to lender, and some lenders will accept borrowers with lower credit score, but charge a higher interest rate on the loan or mortgage. While your personal credit is not as important when buying commercial properties, (both large residential or commercial tenants), lenders still want to see that you don't neglect your monthly payments. (Once again, don't panic—there are ways to partner with people with good credit, which I will describe later.)

Closing costs: When you bought your personal home, your realtor probably told you to make sure you have

2% of the purchase price available for closing costs. This covers legal fees and land transfer tax, and allows you to hire a home inspector. (Never try to cut costs by neglecting the home inspection, even if you are a tradesman. Home inspectors very often check things you would not normally think of.) When buying commercial properties, closing costs are often much higher. Building inspection costs are higher, as the property is usually quite a bit larger; land transfer taxes are larger; legal fees are greater; and then there are the environmental studies and lender's fees to pay. Closing costs for a commercial building can't be estimated as a percentage of the purchase price; instead, it will be more useful to calculate a minimum and a maximum amount for each of the expenses. A wise commercial real estate broker once told me that I should never buy a commercial property worth less than $1.5 million. I didn't understand then, but I certainly do now that I have made this mistake. His point was that closing costs for a $0.5 million property are pretty similar to closing costs for a $1.5 million property, but it takes much longer to earn back the costs with the smaller property.

I would suggest that you look at lots of properties and learn all you can about what's available. You should also be learning more about how to manage the particular property type, too. But before making an offer, you should have a plan for the three items in the list, even if your plan is, "find a partner with money and good credit".

Do you need a real estate agent?

I always hire a real estate agent when I buy properties, and almost always when I sell. When buying a property, it's really a no-brainer, because it doesn't cost any money—the seller pays the agent commission. You have to pick the right agent, though. The right real estate agent understands the buying and selling processes for what you are buying (commercial or residential), he or she has experience in the specific market and knows the market price for the units in the building, and understands the rental profile of the building and the area. The right agent also knows how to help in the negotiating process and is a good source for professionals you will need, from inspectors to lawyers.

When selling properties, I like to have an agent that represents me, and who will arrange all of the advertising and showings. You might like doing that kind of work, and you may be able and willing to do it yourself, but I would rather spend my time and energy on other activities.

Do you need a lawyer to close?

Yes. Even though you are paying for the lawyer, he or she actually works for the mortgage lender, too. Even in the most basic, standard residential purchase, a lawyer must register you on title as the new owner of the property. The lawyer also registers the lender on title to protect the lender's interest in the property. The lender demands that property insurance is in place, and that the lender is listed as a beneficiary on the insurance policy, so the lawyer ensures that you have purchased an insurance policy.

Do you need a corporation?

Most people who own one or two properties, or even more, do not hold their properties in a corporation, but in their personal name.

I opened corporations to hold my properties because I wanted to separate the business from the personal for tax and legal reasons, but the biggest reason was that I was planning, from the beginning, to create a big business.

There are also real estate investors who own hundreds of properties in their personal name.

There is no single right or wrong answer. Talk to your lawyer and accountant to get advice for the right structure for you and your situation.

Do you need a separate bank account?

Even if you decide not to incorporate, I strongly recommend opening a new bank account, and running all of the property income and expenses through only this bank account. Believe me, this will make your annual tax return much easier.

Real Estate Fundamentals

There are some basic numbers to understand before you can speak "real estate". Here is the cash flow formula in its most basic form. This is the starting place to use in calculating whether or not to pursue purchase of a particular property.

Example calculation (all numbers are yearly totals):

Rental income (monthly x 12)	$1000 * 12 = $12000
Minus expenses	- $8000
= Net Operating Income (NOI)	*= $4000*
Minus mortgage cost	- $3000
Profit/Cash flow per year	*= $1000*

If this calculation shows a yearly profit, as this example does, then it may be worthwhile to investigate further.

Before making an offer on the property, consider whether this property fits into your strategy.

If it does (more on this in another chapter) then make an offer, including the requirement for the seller to provide two years of utility bills and maintenance records, and proof of all rents.

DUE DILIGENCE

The real work begins after you have an accepted offer. During the due diligence period, you book a building inspection and environmental studies, as required, and you calculate and re-calculate to ensure that this will be a cashflow-positive property, or you can turn it into one.

The key to getting the calculations right is to use the correct current rents and include ALL of the expenses. Get all of the relevant numbers from the seller, and ensure, as much as is possible, that the expense numbers the seller provides are correct. If the seller is cooperative, you will have copies of at least two years of bills so that you can total the expenses yourself. If the seller is not cooperative, you will have to work much harder to learn the details you need to make a proper analysis. And, If the seller is not cooperative, ask yourself why that might be. Is he or she hiding something that would reduce the perceived value of the property?

The following is not an exhaustive list of possible expenses, but will help to get you thinking about possibilities you may not normally think of.

- Property taxes
- Insurance
- Heat (Gas or Oil)
- Electricity
- Water/Sewer
- Water heater rental
- Garbage removal
- Snow removal

- Grass cutting
- Bookkeeping/Accounting/Tax preparation
- Maintenance/Repairs
- Management (on-site or off-site)
- Advertising (for tenants)
- Vacancy loss (to account for vacant months)

Also include the three 5's: add 5% of gross rents for maintenance, 5% of gross rents for management (even if you will be managing the property yourself), and 5% of gross rents for vacancy. The vacancy budget will help you carry the property through times between tenants.

If you own the property in a corporation, you will also have legal and corporate expenses:

- Yearly corporate returns. (Federal returns cost $20/year if you do them on-line. Your lawyer will charge you more than that to do them.)
- Provincial corporate returns. (Not all provinces require yearly returns. New Brunswick charges $200/year, as an example.)
- Yearly corporate minutes (may or may not cost you money)
- Financial statements
- Tax returns

If this all sounds like a lot of work, it is. Do your full due diligence, and don't cut corners, or you could end up with a property that will cause you grief for years.

Rent-to-Own: Another way to invest in real estate

Rent-to-own deals, sometimes called Lease Options, are an old, but new again way of buying and selling rental real estate. The idea is that families who cannot get approved for a mortgage can get into their own home a few years early, by renting it with an option to buy it at a later date. This is a more expensive option for the tenant-buyer, and there are two questions I am frequently asked:

- Why would a tenant-buyer want to buy through the rent-to-own process rather than waiting until they can get a mortgage?

- Why would an investor want to participate in a rental agreement with a person with credit so bad that he or she cannot get a mortgage?

Tenant-buyers are like everyone else. They are not patient. They are fully aware that they have messed up their own credit, although they aren't always sure how, but they still want to buy a house. They often come to rent-to-own through their mortgage broker. The mortgage broker has tried every lender they know, but has not found someone willing to lend to their client. As a last-ditch effort, they find a rent-to-own investor, or a rent-to-own company who is willing to take a chance on their client. After all this work with their mortgage broker, the clients are no longer thinking about renting at all. They have usually already chosen a house, and that's all they can see. Although it is explained to them that they will be paying more in the long run, all they can see is that this is a way to get the house they already think of as their own.

On the investor side, there are many advantages to the rent-to-own model. First, the tenant-buyer must provide a deposit, sometimes called an option fee, similar to a down-payment. In some cases, this deposit may be as low as two or three thousand dollars, but it is sometimes as large as 20% of the house purchase price. In addition, there is an option fee added to the rent every month. In many urban markets in Canada, this additional option fee makes the difference between the property making a monthly profit and not making a profit. This explains why the rent-to-own option is so attractive to many investors.

TENANT-BUYER PROFILE

In more detail, the tenant-buyers usually have the following attributes:

Poor credit: Some of the reasons tenants give for their poor credit are divorce, illness and job loss. Looking at their credit reports, we can also see evidence of poor spending habits. With some tenants, it's pretty easy to tell that they want more stuff than they can afford. In other cases, the tenants are generous to a fault, and they give their money away to help family members rather than paying their bills.

No credit: In some cases, the tenant-buyers are too young to have built a credit history, or they are new immigrants to Canada and they have no credit history in Canada yet.

Self-employed: Most lenders need self-employed borrowers to show at least two years (with some lenders it's three years) of history in the business. If the tenant-buyer has been in business fewer than two years, they are often declined by lenders.

Insufficient down payment: Some tenant-buyers have a decent credit record rating, but they don't yet have the full down payment saved up. Many rent-to-own investors will start a rent-to-own with less than 10% down.

COMPARING RENT-TO-OWN TO OTHER REAL ESTATE INVESTMENTS

A rent-to-own investment includes the same profit centres as for other real estate investments, with three important differences.

Tenant-buyer deposit

The deposit may not immediately sound like profit centre, but it actually is, since the investor can use these funds as a contingency fund, or even towards the next purchase. There is often confusion about this, and the next section—Additional Cash Flow—describes why this is so.

Additional Cash Flow

The cash flow is much higher in rent-to-own investments because the tenant-buyer pays a "savings" portion in addition to the market rent. From a tenant-buyer's perspective, one of the important benefits of rent-to-own is that they don't have to have a full down-payment, or if they do, they will have an even higher down payment at the end of the rent-to-own.

By the time the tenant-buyer purchases the property, they have a down payment that is the total of:

Deposit + (Savings portion * months) = *Down payment*

The savings portion of the monthly lease payment is one of the biggest sources of confusion to investors learning about rent-to-own for two reasons. First, the investor and the tenant-buyer have different views of the savings portion of the payment, and second, there is always confusion over how the savings portion is paid back to the tenant-buyer at purchase time.

Here is an example to show how it works:

House price: $200,000

Tenant-buyer deposit: $10,000

Term: 3 years

Market rent:
$1200/month

Savings portion:
$200/month

Total rent:
$1400/month

Savings at the end of 3 years (36 months):

Deposit + (Savings portion * months) = Down payment

$$\$10,000 + (200 * 36) = \mathbf{\$17,200}$$

For the tenant-buyer, this is forced savings toward their purchase.

Investors often wonder whether they must keep the $200 per month in an account somewhere so that it is available to give back to the tenant-buyer at the end of the three years. That is not necessary. When the purchase agreement is written, a Schedule is added to the purchase contract. In this Schedule, the savings calculation is itemized, and the savings portion—the $17,200—is credited to the tenant-buyer towards the purchase. No cash changes hands at this point; it's only a credit.

So, for the investor, the savings portion—the $200 per month—is additional cash flow.

Some lenders require a cash down payment that comes directly from the tenant-buyer, so when the tenant-buyer is ready to purchase the home, they must work with a mortgage broker who knows which lenders to approach to make sure that the down payment can be credited in this way.

Some real estate lawyers are unfamiliar with this model, so it's a good idea to ask around for a lawyer who is comfortable with closing rent-to-own purchases. It will make your life much easier if you don't have to train your lawyer in rent-to-own.

Little or no maintenance cost

Most rent-to-own agreements include clauses requiring that tenant-buyers do all the maintenance of the property, including paying for it. This makes rent-to-own properties the easiest to manage.

In some cases, the agreement requires that the tenant pay the first $500 or $1000 of any repair item, with the investor paying the balance each time.

No earned appreciation

One of the things I like best about rent-to-own is that the profit in the investment can be completely calculated from the beginning.

The returns are predictable because the selling price is determined up-front, based on your realtor's prediction of market growth in your area during the term of the rent-to-own. In a three year deal in Halifax, for example, you and your realtor may look at the market, and decide that the houses in your market are likely to increase by 2% per year. The market appreciation is likely to be different in every city, and will also change depending on the neighbourhood the house is in.

Continuing with our previous example, and assuming that the house is in Halifax, the price your tenant-buyer will pay in three years will be:

$200,000 + 2% + 2% + 2% = $212,241.60

If the market price is higher than that at the end of three years, the tenant still buys the house for $212,241.60.

If the tenant adds a garage, develops the basement, and landscapes the entire lot, the tenant still pays you $212,241.60.

I personally don't mind this. I am very happy that the tenants love the house, and are committed to it. That tells me that they are very likely to purchase the house at the end of the term, and that protects my investment.

Increased value of the house also means that it is easier for the tenants to get a mortgage, because the house appraises at a higher value.

And if the rent-to-own fails, you will have a more valuable house to sell.

Additional advantages

In addition to predictable returns, you also have a pre-determined exit strategy. Although it's always good to have a Plan B, when you have a properly-purchased property and a properly qualified rent-to-own tenant, you probably won't need the Plan B.

Rent-to-own is one of the least labour-intensive ways to invest in real estate, since the tenant:

- Pays all the utility bills
- Fixes the toilet (and pays for anything else that goes wrong)
- Replaces the roof
- Shovels the driveway
- Cuts the grass

I specialized in rent-to-own to build my wealth because I was working full-time. I didn't have time for all the babysitting involved in standard landlording. In a rent-to-own investment, the investor only has to:

- Pay the insurance
- Pay the property taxes
- Pay the mortgage
- Make sure the rent arrives on schedule

Make sure the tenant-buyers are on track to improve their credit enough to be able to buy the house at the end of the term.

Because the tenant-buyer is committed to the house, he or she is proud of it, and is more likely to keep it clean and well-maintained. Some tenant-buyers also make significant investments in renovating and improving the house and yard. I encourage these renovations and improvements because they help to tie the tenant-buyer to the property. I remind them that, by making improvements, they are increasing the value of the house, and since their purchase price will not change, it will be easier to get a mortgage when it's time for them to buy the house.

Another reason this is good for the investor is that if the tenant-buyer backs out for any reason, the renovations are likely to make the property easier to sell.

Disadvantages and risks

In many urban markets in Canada, rent-to-own is an attractive strategy because it is difficult to get cash flow from standard rental properties. The additional rent/savings portion often makes the difference between profit and loss (assuming that you are buying with the minimum down payment).

This is great as long as your tenant-buyer stays to complete the purchase of the house at the end of the rent-to-own term.

If the tenant leaves before the end of the term, you can sell the house, find a new rent-to-own tenant, or find a standard renter. A standard renter won't be paying the savings portion, so, depending on what you paid for the house, and how it was financed, it might mean that you will lose money every month.

If you have to sell the house, then you will really appreciate having purchased a good house in a good and growing market.

If the tenant stops paying rent, you can evict them. Make sure you have the right contracts for the province so that you can enforce your landlord rights if the tenant-buyer breaks the contract.

TYPES OF RENT-TO-OWN

There are many variations of rent-to-own, but there are two primary categories: Tenant-first and Property-first.

Tenant-first

In the tenant-first model, the tenant-buyer is qualified first. After the tenant has passed all the tests, and been qualified by your mortgage broker, you send the tenant out with a realtor to find a house. The mortgage broker will provide a maximum price for the house, and suggest a term for the rent-to-own contract, based on how long it will take for the tenant-buyers' financial problems to be resolved to a point where they will be able to get a mortgage.

In my opinion, the primary benefit of the tenant-first model is that the tenant-buyer becomes emotionally attached to the house during the seeking and purchase process, and is less likely to leave the rent-to-own agreement before the end of the term. Tenant-buyers who are attached to their homes are also more likely to maintain and make improvements to the property.

Property-first

In the property-first model, a house is purchased first, in a neighbourhood you know good tenants will want to live in and subsequently buy. The primary advantage to this model is that you are more likely to be able to buy at a discount because you do not have to consider the wishes of a particular tenant-buyer. You are also more likely to be able to specify a high-growth neighbourhood, although you can also be quite prescriptive about the neighbourhood and house specification in the tenant-first model, if you choose to be.

The biggest disadvantage to this model is that, unless you have a list of qualified tenant-buyers who want to live in your chosen neighbourhood and house, you could end up paying the carrying costs on an empty house until you are able to find the right tenant.

REFUNDABLE VS. NON-REFUNDABLE DEPOSIT

When I was first introduced to rent-to-own, I was told that one of the really attractive characteristics was that the tenant-buyer deposit is non-refundable. With a non-refundable deposit, if the tenant-buyer leaves the deal without purchasing the property, the investor is able to keep the deposit. This is very useful in that the deposit is available to help with property carrying costs until the property is sold or re-rented. Unfortunately, this encouraged a few dishonest investors to place unqualified tenant-buyers in homes, so that the deal would fail and the investor could keep the deposit. The investor would then write a new rent-to-own agreement with the next unqualified tenant-buyer, and once again keep the deposit when the deal failed.

Although most investors are honest, it's the dishonest ones who appear on the news.

Along with the many mortgage rule changes in the period after the US housing crash, Canada Mortgage and Housing Corporation (CMHC) started looking closely at rent-to-own agreements before agreeing to insure tenant-buyer mortgages, and they took a distinct dislike to the non-refundable clause. Many conscientious investors have moved with this change and are no longer making the deposit non-refundable.

In the agreements I have used most recently, the deposit was refundable, but only after the house is sold. All selling costs are deducted before the deposit is returned. This strikes me as fair, since with the tenant-buyer defaulting on the agreement, the planned profits are lost, but at least the costs of wrapping up the deal are covered.

CHOOSING GOOD TENANTS AND GOOD PROPERTIES

Here are a few of the questions you should ask in qualifying tenant-buyers for the rent-to-own investment:

Are all of the adults working and in stable jobs? If

the potential tenant-buyer is in a seasonal job like construction or snow plowing, how will he or she pay rent
in the off-season? How long has he or she been in their
current job?

**If one or more of the tenants lose their jobs, are
there similar jobs within easy commuting distance
from the house?** For example, if the prospective tenant-
buyer works in a hospital as a therapist or x-ray
technician, is there another hospital or medical centre
that can use their skills? If the tenant works in construction,
is there likely to be continued growth in new construction?

**If the tenant has poor credit, are his or her habits
likely to continue to cause trouble?** Can his or her
credit be "fixed" in the time you have set for the rent-
to-own contract? It can be quite difficult to judge this,
but there are clues, both in the tenant-buyer's credit
report and the tenant's story. I always insist on the
tenant writing or telling me the story of how they got
into the trouble that is preventing them from buying a
house. Sometimes the problem is a job loss, and they
are now working again, or sometimes their finances
were ruined by a long illness. If these problems appear
to be resolved, then the tenants-buyers may prove to be
a good risk. If, on the other hand, you can see from
the credit report that the problem is out-of-control
consumption, then you must judge whether the
applicants are likely to be able to change their ways

enough to make on-time rent payments AND be able to get a mortgage at the end of the rent-to-own term.

If there is more than one adult tenant, is their relationship stable? I've been told that the most common reason for failure of a rent-to-own deal is the tenants' marriage failing. In fact, I have had only one of my many rent-to-own deals fail, and it was because of a marriage break-down. It is often very difficult, from the outside, to tell whether a marriage is stable, but occasionally, it's obvious. I was once pitched a rent-to-own deal for a couple who were separated, but who had decided to move in together again because neither of them could afford to live on his or her own. Not a good risk, to my mind.

Occasionally, friends, roommates or siblings want to go into a rent-to-own agreement together. While these arrangements might work, the likelihood is that one of the parties will want to marry or move for work, and then the rent-to-own arrangement will fall apart, and everyone will lose money. I tend to refuse these, too.

One caveat to this rule: In some cultures, families expect to live together as adults and stick together no matter what. Often adult children expect to help their parents and siblings for the duration. If this appears to be the situation, I recommend asking more questions, and being open to changing your mind if the family unit appears to be very stable.

Along with these rules-of-thumb, thorough checking is still required, including credit checks, proof of employment and income, reference checks, and so on.

I know an investor whose primary way of qualifying tenants was to look them in the eye over the kitchen table. In one of his RTO properties, after less than three years, he was already putting his third tenant-buyer family into one of his investment houses. To be fair, this investor was trusting the recommendations of a mortgage broker who was clearly referring less-than-qualified tenant-buyers. Ultimately, of course, it is the investor's responsibility to ensure that full qualification takes place.

CHOOSING GOOD PROPERTIES

Even in the tenant-first model, the investor must retain control of the house-buying process. In a perfect world, if you put a great deal of attention into choosing an excellent tenant, then it shouldn't matter what property the tenant-buyer chooses, right? Unfortunately, unexpected things can happen with even the best and most-committed tenant-buyers, including divorce, illness, or job transfers.

Because there are life events I can't predict, I know I may have to be ready to sell the house, so I have a long list of rules for any house that I buy.

The primary purpose of the rules is that the house must be easy to sell quickly. The house must be urban, and it must be in an attractive—middle-class or better—neighbourhood.

How can I invest if I have no money?

This is the most common question beginner—and even more experienced—investors ask. To most people, this seems completely insurmountable.

There are fast ways to get money, and there are slow ways to do it. The fastest way might be to rob a bank, but that is probably also the riskiest.

This chapter describes many ways to gather up the money to buy real estate. Some are easy, and some are difficult. Some need a lot of know-how, and some need very little.

The first and easiest is to use money you have access to now. I know what you are thinking: "If I had money now, I wouldn't be reading this chapter!" But as the bank ad says, "You may be richer than you think".

MONEY I HAVE NOW

Believe it or not, you may have access to money you haven't thought of yet.

> **Cash:** The first place most people look for money is in their savings account. What I have learned is that a very large proportion of Canadians don't have significant savings accounts.

But someone you know well—family or friends—may be sitting on some cash they simply don't know what to do with, and they may be willing to partner with you in an investment that you will manage. In this case, you must have something to offer that your partner does not—knowledge of how to invest in real estate, for example.

Keep in mind that borrowing from or partnering with family and friends to purchase investment assets is fraught with danger and can damage relationships, so it is very important to have very well thought-out agreements signed, preferably prepared with the help of a lawyer. The agreement defines who contributes what, and how profits will be divided, along with what will happen in each of many different scenarios. The contents of good joint venture agreements are described elsewhere in this book.

RRSP: Did you know that you can use your RRSP to buy real estate? There are rules and limitations, of course, and these are covered in the upcoming RRSP chapter.

Line of Credit (LOC): Lines of Credit allow you to access capital up to a limit, while paying interest only on the amount you are using. The interest is generally much less than you will pay on credit cards, so a line of credit is an excellent resource.

Lines of Credit can be secured or unsecured. A secured line of credit is one that is linked to something of value that is used as collateral, often a property you own. This may be a Home Equity LOC, as described below.

An unsecured line of credit is just a loan, but one that you can pay down and then draw on again, up to a set amount.

As long as your investment is producing a higher return than the interest you are paying on the LOC, investing with your LOC can be a good idea. For example, if the interest rate on your LOC is 3% and your investment produces an 8% return, then you are still making a 5% profit on your investment.

Home Equity Line of Credit (HELOC): The Home Equity Line of Credit is a way to borrow against the equity in your home. Many lenders offer this kind of lending vehicle, but read the rules carefully and ask lots of questions to make sure you have a complete under-standing of how their particular HELOC works. Insist that your banker explain everything in enough detail to satisfy you.

Suppose you own your home, free and clear. The maximum allowable loan amount (current Government of Canada rules) is equal to 80% of the value of your home, so if your house is worth $400,000, then the value of your HELOC would be $320,000, if you own your house free and clear.

If, however, you still owed $250,000 on your mortgage, you would be able to borrow $70,000 ($320,000-$250,000). The really interesting thing about these HELOCs is that you automatically have more borrowing room with every mortgage payment you make.

Private loans: When you have some experience investing, you will also have access to private money from people who lend money as a business. Private lenders are those who are not linked to any bank or finance company, and are lending simply as individuals. You may have to have a strong track record to gain access to this kind of money, and it is often more expensive to borrow. If you don't have a track record, you may still be able to access private money, but it can be much more expensive.

Private loans are sometimes possible from private individuals who agree to lend money to people they like and trust, so cultivate your network so that you meet people like this. They may also charge less than the professional private lenders do.

As described in an earlier chapter, private loans can be secured or unsecured, or they may be structured as a formal mortgage. The nice thing about private loans and mortgages is that you don't usually have to submit to the onerous qualification process required by institutional lenders.

Contrary to what most people think, nearly all active investors run out of money eventually—even people who start out with money. When the investment fund is all tied up in investments, then there is no more money to invest, and you will need to find or raise money.

I'd love to tell you a sure-fire way to find money for investing, but unfortunately, there is no silver bullet. Serious real estate investors and business people almost always end up partnering with other investors eventually.

PARTNERING YOUR SKILLS WITH THE MONEY OF OTHERS

The bottom line about partnering is that you really need either time and skills or money. If you have no money, there is really no reason to partner with another investor who has no money. And if you have no money, you must be prepared to use your skills, and usually, plenty of your time as well.

Assignments

Assignments are a way to generate the money for investing. At its most basic level, to do an assignment, you find and negotiate a property purchase contract, and then sell the contract to a real estate investor before closing day.

The trick to assignments, if there is one, is that you should start with a list of investors looking for properties, and then find exactly the types of properties they are looking for, in the areas they want to buy in.

In addition, it's not enough to find a property on MLS, and put an offer in. No one will pay you for something they can easily do themselves. You have to be able to offer investors deals with significant discounts built in.

This will be clearer with an example. Let's say you find a property listed at $400,000. You put an offer in at $300,000, and get it under contract for $320,000. You offer it to your investor list, and ask for a fee of $5000. If this property is of the type your investors are looking for, and the property is actually worth $400,000, then you will have a happy investor who will be very willing to pay your $5000 fee.

If, on the other hand, you see the $400,000 property and you negotiate a price of $380,000, and still ask for your $5000 fee, your investors are unlikely to be very interested, since this kind of reduction is something they could probably have easily negotiated themselves. Why would they want to lower their profit by $5000 by paying you?

In addition to requiring lots of time and leg-work, you can see that this strategy requires some good skills, especially in negotiation.

Joint Venture Agreements (JVs)

Many investors start their investing careers by joining forces with a partner who has money, but who doesn't want to invest on their own, or doesn't have the time to find and manage a property.

This is an opportunity for you to find someone with skills and assets that are different from yours. Many people gravitate to partners who are very like themselves, but that's not the best way to create a workable venture. For example, if neither of you has money or neither of you has the skills or experience to purchase and manage real esate, you won't get very far.

In the classic real estate joint venture, one partner has the property under contract, and the other(s) have money for the down payment. As with partnering with family and friends, it is very important to have a legal agreement that defines the terms, conditions and time frame for the joint venture.

While complimentary skills and assets are very important to the success of a joint venture, the most important thing about choosing an investing partner is to make sure that their goals and philosophy mesh with yours. You will experience no end of grief if, after signing the JV agreement, you find out that your partner expects their money back in one year, while you have lined up a ten-year project. Worse yet, you could find yourself in an agreement with someone who is willing to do less than fully legal things to increase returns.

And remember, a joint venture contract is any arrangement that you and your partner(s) agree and sign off on. Everything, including who does what, and what the profit sharing proportions are, should be negotiated.

Details about what should be covered in a good joint venture agreement are covered in an earlier chapter.

Slow and steady

Slow and steady saving and investing is out of fashion, but sometimes it's the only way to move forward.

Robert Kiyosaki—"Rich Dad"—has put forward many good ideas in his books. One that I thoroughly endorse, and follow myself, is the idea of putting aside money every day (or every week, or every paycheck) in three jars, or three bank accounts.

Label the jars or accounts "Savings", "Charity" and "Investing". These will cover your three most important responsibilities; having a four-month emergency fund, helping others, and creating an investment fund.

To accelerate your ability to invest, you could also consider taking a second job. After you have finished creating your four- month emergency fund and put aside money for charity, you could put the remainder into your investment fund.

Although this may seem like a slow way to raise the money for investing, slow is better than not at all.

RRSP Mortgages: Lending and Borrowing

Many Canadians know the importance of saving for eventual retirement, and many do contribute to registered retirement savings plans, even if only for the tax deduction.

And most Canadians know that their RRSP should be invested in something, but most don't know how to choose, so they allow their friendly neighbourhood banker to choose for them. I would venture to say that most RRSPs are invested this way, which means that most RRSPs are invested in mutual funds that are sold and managed by the bank. The bank then charges you fees for the privilege of investing in their mutual funds, whether you make a profit or not.

While fees of some kind are expected, you should know that Canadians pay more in mutual fund fees than in almost every other country. The fees can add up to as much as 2.3%, and by the time front-end fees and back-end fees and transaction fees are paid, your advertised 5% return is down to 2.7%. If the central bank is successful in keeping the inflation rate at about 2%, then the return in your RRSP is a very unimpressive 0.7% (5%-2.3%-2% inflation).

This made me think I should find another way to invest the money in my RRSP.

INVESTING YOUR RRSP IN MORTGAGES

When I talk about RRSPs in this chapter, I really mean the full range of registered funds, including:

• RRSP

• LIRA

• RRIF

• RESP

• TSFA

You can hold many different kinds of investments in registered funds:

• Stocks and mutual funds

• Bonds and debentures

• Term deposits and CGIC

• Gold and silver certificates

• Mortgages secured by real property (Canadian property only)

This chapter concentrates on investing your RRSP funds in mortgages.

There are two kinds of RRSP mortgages defined by the Canadian Revenue Agency (CRA), Arm's length, and non-Arm's length. Both are administered by a trustee. Practically speaking, the trustee will be a bank or trust company.

Non-arm's length: lending to yourself, your immediate family, including adopted children, and common-law spouse. Check the CRA rules for the full list.

Arm's length: lending to anyone else

LENDING YOUR RRSP: ARM'S LENGTH MORTGAGES

This chapter is primarily about Arm's length mortgages. While some financial institutions offer non-Arm's length mortgages in many types of registered funds, there are only three or four financial institutions that do Arm's length mortgages, and Arm's length mortgages are only allowed in RRSPs and TFSAs.

I have talked to many people who are not ready to buy their first (or next) income property. They think this means that they cannot improve their financial situation, and that they must wait until they have saved more down payment money or improved their credit.

In many cases, though, they already have an RRSP, and usually, the RRSP is invested in mutual funds.

While you may not be ready to invest in a property, changing your RRSP to invest in an asset that is performing better will improve your financial situation.

The general steps in lending your RRSP or TFSA are:

1. Talk to your financial advisor about selling your mutual funds. Your advisor is likely to try to talk you out of it,

since their income will stop, but stay strong. There may be extra fees, so make sure you know what the limitations are. There may also be timing issues, so if your advisor tells you that you will incur a penalty if you sell your mutual funds now, you need to weigh the penalty against the returns possible for you with the change to investing in mortgages. Or if you decide to wait until conditions are better, find out the exact date the penalty will become lower or disappear.

2. When your funds have been sold—converted to cash—move your RRSP to a self-directed RRSP (SDRRSP). It must be self-directed for you to invest in mortgages.

3. Find a real estate investor, or an investment-oriented mortgage broker you trust, and ask about investing in RRSP mortgages.

4. Negotiate the interest rate and terms with the borrower. The terms include things like payment frequency, term of the mortgage, NSF fees, interest-only vs. principle and interest, and who pays the trustee fees. Your mortgage broker will be able to advise you on these items.

5. Investigate the property and the borrower, and be prepared to pay a lawyer for help if there is information you are unable to get on your own.

6. Fill in and sign the paperwork to complete the mortgage.

7. Over the life of the mortgage, monitor to make sure the payments are coming in as agreed.

What to look for in a safe RRSP mortgage

Choosing a safe RRSP mortgage is very similar to choosing a safe rental property to buy. Ask yourself these questions and ask your mortgage broker or lawyer to help you get the answers, if you can't get them yourself.

How much is the property worth? I recommend that you pay for an appraisal (or have the borrower pay for one) if there isn't a current one.

How much does the borrower already owe on the property? Your lawyer or mortgage broker will be able to get this information because mortgages are registered on the property title.

Does the property produce enough income to make payments on all the debts, including the loan you are considering making? If it is a rental, is it fully occupied?

What do you know about the borrower? Try to find out something about his or her reputation, without divulging any personal information about them, of course. Ask the person who referred the borrower about the borrower's reliability, and so on. You might also consider asking the borrower for references.

If you have trouble getting enough information to make an informed decision, consider asking the borrower to give you a copy of his or her credit report, or ask for permission to have your mortgage broker look it up. I also recommend having your lawyer pull available records about the property and borrower.

It may cost you money in legal and appraisal fees to get all the information you need, but consider how much it could cost you if you go in blind.

If you would like to read a very good book on the topic, I highly recommend The RRSP Secret by Greg Habstritt.

There are many advantages to lending your RRSP in arm's length mortgages, and also a few disadvantages.

Advantages

- Flexible and negotiable interest rates, and the rates are almost always higher than bank mortgage rates.
- The borrower will usually pay all the fees. (You can make this one of the terms of the mortgage.)
- The Trustee automatically takes the payment from the borrower's account, and deposits it into your RRSP.
- Your RRSP grows tax free.
- Predictable investment — you know exactly what your yearly returns will be.
- The returns are almost always better than mutual funds returns, and the fees are often less (in terms of a percentage of the investment).
- You can foreclose on the property if payments stop.

- The mortgage is secured by real estate, so its value is unlikely to ever go down to zero.

Disadvantages

The Trustee (the bank) does not qualify the borrower; this is your responsibility.

The Trustee will notify you if the borrower misses a payment, but does not take action; this is your responsibility.

Very few banks will act as Trustee. Currently only these institutions will act as trustee for RRSP mortgages:

- Olympia Trust
- Canadian Western Trust
- B2B Trust (a division of Laurentian Bank)
- TD Waterhouse (non-arm's length only)

WHAT YOU NEED TO KNOW ABOUT NEGOTIATING RRSP MORTGAGES

RRSP mortgages are the same as standard bank mortgages in many ways, especially in legal terms, but there are also differences that may work to your advantage. Once again, it is up to you to make the mortgage conform to your risk tolerance. If you are unable to do this, you should walk away from the investment.

Here are some of the differences:

Interest rate – arm's length mortgages

As mentioned earlier, the interest the borrower will pay you is not linked to the bank rate in any way, so you can charge any rate you can negotiate. In Canada, any interest rates over 60% are criminal, but the RRSP mortgage trustee is likely to set a limit well below that. With the institution I used, I was allowed to charge up to 30%, but check with the bank you are working with for their rules.

Note that non-arm's length RRSP mortgage interest rates are generally much closer to bank rates than arm's length mortgages.

In practice, private lending rates for mortgages fall into the following ranges. There are exceptions, of course, because these are negotiated between you and the borrower, and they depend on real and perceived risk, and real and perceived need.

- 1st mortgage: 4-8%
- 2nd mortgage: 8-20%
- 3rd mortgage: 15-30%

Loan to Value (LTV)

Unlike the mortgages you can get at conventional lenders, you may be able to arrange mortgages for the full value of the property (100% LTV) with some RRSP trustees. The important question is: Should you?

If the property is 100% financed, and something goes wrong, you are almost certain to lose at least part of your investment. I recommend lending a maximum of 80-90% of the value of the property, but if you choose to lend 100% of the property value, then you are entitled to charge a higher rate, based on the higher risk.

My advice is to set the maximum LTV you are comfortable with, and then not to lend on any higher LTV than that.

For example, if you are lending on a property that is appraised at $200,000, I generally wouldn't lend more than 80% of the value; the maximum I would agree to lend would be $160,000.

Property location

There are two main location considerations. First, the current list of trustees will allow RRSP mortgages on any Canadian property, in all provinces except for Quebec.

Second, consider the location of the property using the same criteria you would use to decide whether the property is a good rental property. For example, ask yourself the following questions, and research the answers:

- If the tenants leave, is there an abundance of other tenants to take their place?

- Are people and businesses moving into the area, or out of it?

- Are the property values in the area going up, or are they going down?

Trustee rules

Trustees allow 1st, 2nd and 3rd mortgages; most real estate investors are looking for 2nd mortgages.

If you consider lending a 2nd mortgage, make sure that the first mortgage lender allows 2nd mortgages—many institutional lenders don't.

Where to find an investor to lend your RRSP to

The best places to find good investors to lend to are your mortgage broker and your local real estate club.

Just remember, no matter where the lead comes from, even if the investor is recommended by your mortgage broker, or is a member of a respected investment group like the Real Estate Investment Network (REIN), for example, you must still do your own due diligence. Make sure that the property is viable and cash flowing, and that the appraised value supports all of the mortgages proposed. Have your mortgage broker check out the borrower. (Get permission from the borrower first.)

A mortgage commitment

Ask your mortgage broker to help you create a formal mortgage commitment. A mortgage commitment is a document that lenders create to put all of the mortgage conditions and rules in. Have your mortgage commitment set out at least the following details:

- Dollar amount of the mortgage
- The property the mortgage will be registered against
- Borrower name, address and phone number
- Interest rate
- Term (number of years)
- Payment frequency – monthly, quarterly, yearly, or only at the end of the term
- Whether the payments will be principle and interest (P&I) or interest only
- Whether or not extensions will be allowed at the end of the term
- NSF fee – If this is not specified, you may have to chase the borrower to reimburse the bank penalty you will be charged if the payment bounces, so it is better to specify a value. Make it large, at least $200 per instance, to make it unpleasant for the borrower and so that they avoid NSFs very carefully.
- Whether there will be an opening and/or closing fee, and the value
- Whether or not there will be a fee for closing out the mortgage early, and what it will be

Talk to your mortgage broker for recommendations on these conditions, and have the borrower sign the document before signing the paperwork that allows your RRSP trustee to advance the money.

Property and Tenant Management

The biggest fears people have about owning investment property are managing the property and getting good tenants. Some landlords call it "Tenants and Toilets". I'm not sure why people are always fixated on toilets, given all of the other challenging things that can happen.

Stereotypical or not, it really is about managing the tenants, and managing the physical property.

TENANT MANAGEMENT

Tenants are your most important clients, because they pay your mortgage. Value your tenants and treat them well; keeping your tenants happy is very important to the smooth running of your building and your business. This section discusses how to get good tenants, and how to keep them.

Know the rules

This is the most important thing of all. Learn the Landlord-Tenant Act for the province where the property is located.

The provincial rules are enforced by the Landlord Tenant Board or Rentalsman for the province. In Ontario, landlords and tenants are governed by the Landlord and Tenant Act, while Nova Scotia and New Brunswick each have a Rentalsman. The legislation has different names in different provinces, and the rules also differ by province, so make sure you know the basics before you sign with your first tenant.

Some of the differences between provinces include things like these:

- In some provinces, you can collect Security Deposit and Damage Deposit, while in others you can collect only Last Month's Rent or half of Last Month's Rent. Some provinces also specify the amounts allowed, and the interest rate to be paid on any money the landlord is holding for deposits and last month's rent.

- Some provinces have rent controls, while others allow the landlord to raise the rent to market rent once a year.

- Some provinces — Ontario is an example — have comprehensive websites, and official forms and procedures the landlord must use for everything from starting and ending lease terms, late rent and evictions, and notice terms. Some provinces also require the use of the standard lease form, and no other lease forms are legal.

- There are also differences with respect to what happens at the end of the lease term. In Ontario, when the lease ends, the tenancy automatically changes over to a month-to-month lease. In Québec, the one year lease automatically renews and becomes another one year lease. Québec also has an interesting convention about moving day—tradition has it that moving day is July 1st.

The most important rule in tenant management is to treat your tenants like the human beings they are.

The second most important rule is that you must understand the rules better than your tenants do. The alternative is having the (rare) bad tenants using the rules against you. In some provinces — Ontario again—a tenant can stay for months without paying rent if you don't respond correctly at the first sign of trouble.

Advertising the vacant unit

How you advertise vacant units determines everything from the type of tenants you attract, to how long it takes to fill the unit.

Know who your desired tenants are (families, students, professionals) and advertise where they are looking. Kijiji works for lots of groups, and if you are advertising for students, you can also advertise on the university or college website, and put up posters on campus and in shops students frequent. If you have a high-end house or condo, you may use MLS and a real estate agent. If you are renting an executive house or condominium for short term stays, you could use an executive rental agency.

Check Kijiji.com for your area, and ads in the newspapers and university ad boards, to find out what units similar to yours in the same area are rented for. You might also call other landlords to ask what their similar units are renting for.

Keep to market rents or just under, to avoid creating or stretching a vacancy.

Include lots of photos, and sell the sizzle by describing the amenities and the neighbourhood, and what's great about living there.

Showing the apartment and taking applications

Make sure to see ID and get the birthdate and current and previous addresses of the prospective tenants. The Social Insurance Number (SIN) makes the credit check easier, but it's not required. Many potential tenants don't mind supplying their SIN, but if they choose not to, you cannot demand it. Consider asking for a job letter from the applicant's employer. Make sure you get the name and number for current and previous landlords.

Call the applicant's employer, and all of the references. Pay special attention to what the previous landlord says. The current landlord may be reluctant to tell the truth (if he or she is hoping to get rid of the tenant) but the previous landlord may be more forthcoming. The large landlords like Minto won't give references, but they will confirm that they have or had the tenant in one of their buildings.

Choosing the tenant

Call all the references, and check the tenant's credit using a service like Rent Check (www.rentcheckcorp.ca) or Tenant

Verification Service, Inc. (www.tenantverification.com)

Confirm that the tenant's take-home pay is at least double, and preferably triple, the monthly lease amount, especially if the tenant will be paying the utilities, too. If the rent is too high for the tenant's income, you and the tenant will both be unhappy because the tenant is very likely to run into financial difficulties that result in missing rent payments.

Preparing and signing the lease, and communicating the rules to the tenant

Make sure the lease covers your rules, but also be aware of the landlord-tenant rules in your province.

In some provinces (Nova Scotia, for example) you must use the standard lease. In Alberta, there are very few rules, while in Ontario, you can put anything you like in your lease, but any clauses that contravene the Landlord-Tenant Act cannot be enforced.

I created a Tenant Binder that I go through with each tenant when we sign the lease. It includes emergency contact information, property management contact info, plus forms for reporting problems and requesting repairs. In Ontario, there are standard information sheets that must be provided to the tenant, so the tenant binder includes them. Check the rental rules for your province to ensure that you know what you need to provide. I also include the names of local insurance agents and require that tenants insure their furniture and belongings. After everyone signs the lease, the lease also goes into the tenant binder.

In Ontario, it is an offense not to have working smoke and carbon monoxide detectors, and the landlord is liable even if the tenant removes or disconnects the smoke detector, so I have the tenant sign a smoke alarm/CO detector form in which they promise to keep it in working order. This also goes into the Tenant Binder.

Tour the unit with the tenant, and take photos to confirm the condition of the unit while filling in an inspection report. You and the tenant will sign two copies of the report, and you leave one copy of the report with the tenant.

Managing rent collection and the tenant relationship

The value of an investment property is based on the income, so it is important to raise the rent whenever the landlord-tenant act allows, especially in rent control provinces.

Pay attention to the rules for raising the rent and notice periods, and how the notice must be delivered.

If your rent is already at the correct level for the market, you may choose not to raise it, especially if the increase would make it more difficult to rent the unit.

Reward tenants for the behaviour you want

Your tenants are like anyone else; they like to be appreciated. And when you appreciate them as paying clients, which they are, they will generally reward you with on-time payments and respect for your property.

One of the ways to reward on-time payment is to send a small gift every six months to tenants who have paid on time for all six months. In the small-town Ontario market, I send a $20 Tim Horton's gift card to each tenant. That works well for my market, but it may not work for yours. Consider the type of tenant you have, and the retailers they frequent. If you have students in an urban area, you might send gift cards to a local coffee shop, or maybe an iTunes card. If you have older men in your building, a Canadian Tire card might be appreciated. If you have families, a grocery card or a gift certificate for a local restaurant might work well. If you know your tenants and the neighbourhood they live in, you will be able to come up with the right incentive.

One of my mentors has an interesting way of rewarding tenants that they greatly appreciate, and that doesn't add a budget item. At the end of every year, he sends a letter to each tenant who has paid on time for the full year. This letter thanks them for being great tenants and offers them a reward of their choice. The list might include a new fridge, microwave, or stove, or it might include new paint or carpet throughout the house or apartment. The items on the list are already in the budget for that unit in the coming year, so it doesn't cost extra, and tenants are very happy to have their living space upgraded.

For tenants who really would prefer cash, you might choose to rebate some portion of their rent every six months or every year, especially if they do some work at the property for you, like minor repairs or mowing or shovelling. Always pay these directly to the tenant rather than allowing them to pay a lower rent for the month. This makes bookkeeping and accounting much easier because you have a stable rent, with tax-deductible payments for services rendered by the tenants.

One caution: Don't reward your best tenants with rent reductions. The income your rental property is generating is one of the primary determinants of the value of the property, and lower rents means a lower property value when you want to re-finance or sell the property.

The only time to offer a rent reduction is when there is a risk of a good tenant leaving because the rent they are paying is above current market rent.

PROPERTY MANAGEMENT

Maintaining the property is critical to preserving its value, and improvements, renovations and additions are the best way to force appreciation beyond the average in its market.

Preparing the rental unit between tenants

Depending on how long the departing tenant has been in the unit, you may be able to just clean before putting a new tenant in. If the tenant has been in the unit for several years, though, you may have to paint, replace flooring, and possibly appliances. When a long-term tenant leaves, and you are likely to have a month's vacancy anyway, you might decide to replace bigger items, like furnace and windows, or even kitchen and bath.

Some landlords recommend making all updates, including invasive ones, with the tenants in place, to avoid losing a month's rent for renos.

Others have a policy of repainting every year, to keep the unit fresh, but also to get a good look at the unit at least once a year.

Planning for maintenance items

It's important to have money available to fix things that go wrong, for example, a dripping tap, a toilet, a floor tile, and so on, along with funds to pay the handyman or contractor.

It is also good to know the ages of the appliances, including the water heaters, to be able to predict when they will require replacement.

Having a schedule for the water heater(s) is especially important, to make sure that it is replaced before it fails (doing it the other way around means an expensive flood).

Budgeting for building repairs like new roof or furnace

When you buy a property, it's important to know how old the roof and furnace are and when they will need to be replaced. Then you will have to make sure the money is put aside, ready to make the replacements when they are required.

Hiring and supervising contractors

Make sure that you have a ready list of reliable handymen and tradesmen. When purchasing in a new market, take the time to talk to realtors, home inspectors and tenants for referrals to competent and reliable tradesmen. Another great source of names we have found is local hardware store employees.

Budgeting for and purchasing appliances

With electricity costs increasing every year, it is important to have fairly new, energy-efficient appliances, especially the refrigerator and the water heater, whether you or the tenant is paying the bill. If the tenant is paying for the electricity, the affordability of your unit will be affected by high electricity costs, and you may end up having to lower the rent you charge.

Ontario now requires landlords to provide the cost of running the fridge when leasing to new tenants, if they will be paying the electrical bill.

Multiple Income Streams

If we are investing to provide income, then it makes sense to maximize the income streams so that we will be comfortable, and also have a cushion for emergencies. Ideally, by the time we want to retire, we will have enough income for the way we want to live, not only when we first retire, but also to cover whatever care we will need if our health fails.

If we are relying on just one source of income, as most of us do when we are working, we might find ourselves in dire straits if that one source suddenly stops, through job loss, or through bankruptcy of a pension plan.

While this is where our savings account comes in (four months' worth of expenses), it is also wise to have multiple sources of income to cushion the blow, or even to replace the income we have lost.

Before retirement, we might expect to have the following income streams:

- Salary/Commissions
- Dividend income from stocks or Real Estate Income Trusts (REITs)
- Residual income from rental properties

After retirement, we are likely to have some different sources of income:

- Canada Old Age Security

- Canada Pension Plan (CPP)/ Québec Pension Plan (QPP)
- Work-related pensions
- Registered Retirement Income Fund income
- Dividend income from stocks or Real Estate Income Trusts (REITs)
- Residual income from rental properties

If you don't have all of these income sources, or if the combined income at either stage is insufficient, you might consider adding incoÏme streams. The list is limited only by your imagination, but here are a few ideas:

- Renting out a room in your home, either to a permanent tenant or to vacationers
- Renting out a parking space, garage, or storage in your home
- Renting out your back yard to vegetable gardeners
- Using your hobbies—teaching others how to do something you have skill in (arts or crafts, genealogy, bookkeeping, computer skills), or selling your arts and crafts
- Collecting royalties—residual income from patents or books

You may not have all of these income possibilities now, but there are likely to be some of these that you can create over time to prepare for a time when you need the additional income.

As time goes on, you may want to switch more and more to passive types of income, and retain only those active sources that you really enjoy, and would happily do with or without the income.

Conclusion

Y ou don't have to be a financial guru to be able to make hugely beneficial changes to your income, savings, and future lifestyle.

In this book, you learned the difference between active and passive investing, and all of the possibilities in between. You learned how to get started even if you didn't think you had access to any money, and how to invest your RRSP in real estate, even if you thought that money was locked away until you turn 65.

Starting out as an active investor and managing your own properties, this book also serves as a primer and a starting place for your tenant and property relationships.

If you feel inspired, don't wait for the inspiration to die down. Start today by searching for investment groups and clubs in your city. There are sure to be many options, so register for and attend some of them. As you attend each meeting, you may find a group that provides exactly the type of information and contacts you need, and you may not, but either way, you are sure to meet interesting people who could become friends or even investment partners.

As you narrow down to your particular interest, get more involved in your clubs and groups, and learn all you can until you feel ready to decide what kind of investing is right for you. Then, through your groups, find one or two mentors who can advise you or introduce you to the people you will need to take the next step on your chosen path.

It IS possible to retire early, and retire better, and it IS possible to generate the kind of income that will also allow you to take care of those you love when they need you most.

Start by learning about the options and finding experts to help you make your first investments. And by experts, I mean people who are actually doing what they are telling you to do, rather than just sales people at the bank or brokerage.

If you got only one thing out of reading this book, I hope it's that you—yes, YOU—have the ability to take charge of your own financial health.

Go out and get started!

ABOUT THE AUTHOR - ANITA FLEGG

After her divorce a few years ago, Anita became worried about whether she would ever be able to stop working. She had worked for more than twenty years in a professional career, but she had no pension, and she realized that she had no retirement plan. That's where her investment education began. Anita started studying real estate investing; travelling for courses, and hiring coaches. The most important things she has learned are that coaches are the best possible investment, and that there is always more to learn.

This book is part of a challenge Anita was given by her current coaches. Coach Bob challenged Anita to increase her network, socialize more, and start teaching and leading other women to take charge of their own finances. This challenge led directly to the creation of the Boomer Women Invest Meetup group, and from there, to this book. Anita has learned that she loves teaching and coaching other women, and feels blessed to have met so many wonderful people, most of whom she would never have met without her real estate investing career.

Anita spends a lot of time, energy and passion on her investing, but it's a means to an end—not an end in itself. It's a way to allow Anita the resources to travel more, explore music and art, and spend more time with family and friends, in Ottawa and all over the world.

.